HARD TIMES

GROUP BIBLE STUDY

WRITTEN BY Joe Allison

Hard Times: Group Bible Study
Written by Joe Allison
© 2019 Warner Press Inc.

Requests for information should be sent to:
Warner Press Inc.
P.O. Box 2499
Anderson, IN 46018
www.warnerpress.org

Kevin Stiffler • Editor
S. Katie Miller • Layout & Design

CONTENTS

The Warner Press *Relevance* Group Bible Studies provide intriguing examinations of topics using the whole of the Scriptures. The guides incorporate various stories and activities to introduce and apply the subject matter, with a Bible study component at the heart of each session. Our goal is to show life-long believers and those new to the faith how to know the Lord intimately while encouraging them to step out and join him in his work with miraculous results.

These flexible studies are ideal for any setting. We know that time is a valuable commodity in today's society, and that's why each book consists of five or six short lessons intended to meet the group's scheduling needs.

L1

Joseph Taken to Egypt

Genesis 37

Main Point

Hard times helped Joseph discern his destiny, and they can help us in the same way too.

Background

Young Joseph's life was spiraling downward. Though the favorite son of a wealthy man, his brothers sold him into slavery. Falsely accused of sexual assault, he was then confined to a foreign jail. Yet he discovered through these hardships that God could use him to bless other people. That was his destiny. Hard times may fill us with hope or bitterness, depending on our outlook. As the second-century writer Origen said, the same sun that melts the wax hardens the clay. Joseph warmed to God's leading as he grew from a youth to a man through a gauntlet of hard times.

What Would You Like to Know?

Human beings have an intense curiosity about their future, which is why fortune-tellers are still popular in the twenty-first century. Millions consult their horoscopes in daily newspapers. We laugh over slips of paper we extract from fortune cookies, then pocket them for future reference. Most of us would love to know what will happen to us ten or twenty years from now. We especially want to know what the future holds for our material well-being. *Will I have a lucrative career? Will I "marry well"? Will I have robust health and long life?*

What is one sincere question you have about your future? Why does the answer to this question mean so much to you? How might hard times help to answer this question?

____

____

____

____

How does your personal question compare to the questions of others? What commonalities are represented? Why are such things of concern to so many people?

____

____

____

Abraham was Joseph's great-grandfather. What had God promised Abraham concerning the land where Jacob and his family now lived (see Gen 15:18–21)?

If Joseph's father Jacob told his own sons about this promise, how might it have affected their sense of self-worth?

Jacob sent Joseph to help the sons of Bilhah and Zilpah in herding sheep (Gen 35:25–26). Apparently, he was the only brother who did not work on his own. (Their youngest brother, Benjamin, stayed at home.) What might this suggest about Joseph's maturity?

Cite three things in this passage that explain why Joseph's brothers hated him. If you also had a strained relationship with your siblings, what caused it?

Even though Jacob showed favoritism toward Joseph compared to the other brothers, Joseph's dreams apparently upset Jacob. How would you account for this? What does it mean that Jacob "kept the matter in mind" (v 11)?

II. Read Genesis 37:12–24.

Jacob was anxious to know whether his sons fared well because they had taken revenge on Shechem's family for the rape of Dinah a few years earlier (Gen 34). What were the risks of sending Joseph to check on them?

God's people had not yet received the Ten Commandments, so some would argue that Joseph's brothers would not have been guilty of murder if they had left him to die of exposure. Do you agree? Is written law (revealed through the Scriptures) more important than natural law (revealed through human conscience)? Explain.

III. Read Genesis 37:25–30.

One of the brothers convinced the rest to sell Joseph into slavery. What do you think caused them to have second thoughts about killing Joseph? Did they have pity on him or were they simply anxious to avoid punishment? Why do you say so?

Although Reuben was the eldest son, he seems to have been absent when his brothers sold Joseph into slavery; he was distraught to find the cistern empty. Why do you suppose the others didn't seek Reuben's approval of this decision?

IV. Read Genesis 37:31–36.

Jacob jumped to the conclusion that Joseph had been killed by a wild beast. What things had Jacob done in the past that perhaps caused him to expect some sort of violent tragedy to befall his family?

How might the brothers have justified their treatment of Joseph?

How did this turn of events threaten the fulfillment of Joseph's dreams?

The Overcomers

History gives us many powerful stories of people who pursued their dreams despite overwhelming odds. Here are a few such persons:

- Charles W. Naylor, who was bedridden for life by an accident at a revival he was conducting

- Franklin D. Roosevelt, who was stricken by polio while preparing to run for president

- Malala Yousafzai, who was shot by terrorists at age twelve while campaigning for girls' schools

What do you know about the life stories of these persons and the hard times they experienced? Do some research if you can and record pertinent details:

____

____

Why did these people persist in following their dreams despite the tragedies they faced? What other people do you know of whose lives tell similar stories?

____

____

When we face tragedies or hard times, how can we "keep in mind" that God is with us and may be up to something greater than we could imagine?

____

____

Does God Have a Plan for You?

Does God predetermine each person's future, or is the future contingent upon our personal choices and changing circumstances? Joseph's story gives us a good opportunity to explore this question.

Here are some comments overheard in daily conversation. Place a check mark (√) by a statement if you agree with it, an *X* if you disagree with it, and a question mark (?) if you are not sure what you think about it:

______ Everything happens for a reason.

______ It must have been her time (to be promoted, to marry, to die, etc.).

______ Fate loves the fearless.

______ If you do not create your destiny, your fate will be inflicted upon you.

______ God has a wonderful plan for your life.

How do your responses to these statements compare with those of others? With which statements do most people seem to agree? With which ones do most disagree? Why?

Fate vs. Destiny

The words *fate* and *destiny* are not interchangeable. Theologian Georgia Harkness made some helpful distinctions between these terms.[1]

Harkness wrote that *fate* is an impersonal concept; whatever happens simply happens. A fatalist has no good explanation for why something occurs, simply saying that "fate" caused it. Jesus teaches us to accept God's will for our lives, but those with a fatalistic point of view do not submit to the will of an all-knowing God; instead, they submit to a "something" that is vague and impersonal.

Harkness wrote that *destiny* is a personally purposeful future. Its pattern is seldom seen as events happen, but becomes apparent later. A person with a sense of destiny believes the future is at best partially known and does not expect God to reveal detailed information about what will happen.

Which parts of these statements ring true to your experience, and which do not? Which parts seem biblically sound, and which do not? Which parts best agree with what you have been taught in your congregation, and which do not? Explain.

Do you believe Joseph's dreams expressed his fate or his destiny? Which concept do you think is more consistent with Christian faith? Why?

____

____

____

____

____

Closing Prayer

Lord, we want to catch a glimpse of our future. You may give us a dream as you did to Joseph, or speak to us through trusted mentors, or inspire us through the stories of other people who have served you. Help us to know when you are speaking, however you choose to do it. And give us faith to press on toward our best future, despite the obstacles we might face along the way. Amen. ∎

1. See "Providence, Destiny, and Fate," in Georgia Harkness, *The Providence of God* (Nashville: Abingdon, 1960), chap. 2.

Joseph in Prison

Genesis 39 — 40

Main Point

During hard times, Joseph saw that God still cared for him; God cares for us faithfully, as well.

Background

After Joseph was purchased by Potiphar, his master saw what an effective manager he was. Potiphar placed him in charge of everything he owned until his wife falsely accused Joseph of sexual assault. Then Potiphar threw him into prison. There Joseph befriended Pharaoh's former baker and cupbearer. He interpreted their dreams and asked that they remember him when they gained their freedom, but Joseph was left to languish behind bars. This is a common experience of anyone who falls on hard times. Life is lonely at the top, but things can be far lonelier on the bottom! Yet God guides and blesses us, sometimes in very subtle ways.

⌐ How to Respond?

Bill, Jill, and Gil are professional people who work in the same building, but not at the same company. Bill and Jill are standing in line at the coffee shop downstairs when their friend Gil arrives. They chat for a while because they haven't seen one another for months. But when Bill and Jill invite Gil to join them for coffee, they learn that he has lost his job and his home, so he's only here to see if the shop has any jobs open. Gil politely declines their invitation because he doesn't even have enough money for coffee.

How do you imagine the mood of the conversation changing when Gil's story is learned by Bill and Jill? How do you think Gil might feel when it changes? Buying Gil's coffee would be a wonderful thing, but how else could the other two affirm that they are still his friends?

I. Read Genesis 39:1–6a.

Verse 2 says, "The Lᴏʀᴅ was with Joseph so that he prospered." Give a couple of examples of people who were not successful in the ordinary sense, yet you believe God was with them.

Give examples of leaders or businesspeople you know who were blessed because God was with one or more of the people who served under this leader or worked at this company.

Potiphar placed Joseph in charge of his household. What sort of words and actions by Joseph might have convinced Potiphar that he could trust him?

II. Read Genesis 39:6b–20.

Besides Joseph's good looks, what else might have attracted Potiphar's wife to him? How have you seen sexual infidelity cause the downfall of a leader and trouble for the organization that this person led?

Why did Joseph refuse to have sexual relations with Potiphar's wife? How do you think she felt about this, and why?

III. Read Genesis 39:21–23.

If Potiphar had already seen Joseph's success and believed he could trust Joseph, then why did Potiphar believe his wife's accusations? What *could* have been Joseph's punishment at Potiphar's order, and what might this tell us?

How was the jailkeeper's treatment of Joseph similar to Potiphar's treatment of Joseph? What might have convinced the jailer that he could trust Joseph?

IV. Read Genesis 40:1–8.

What might the cupbearer and the baker have done to offend Pharaoh? Does it matter in the larger scheme of this story? Why or why not?

How did Joseph explain to his fellow prisoners his ability to interpret dreams?

What did Joseph risk by interpreting other prisoners' dreams? Why did he do it?

V. Read Genesis 40:9–23.

Joseph told both the baker and the cupbearer that Pharaoh would "lift your head," but this meant something very different for each of them! Recall a time when a friend warned that you were headed for trouble. How did you respond? Are you more or less likely to believe a friend who is already in trouble? Why?

How might things have turned out differently if God was *not* with Joseph when his brothers captured him? when Potiphar threw him in prison? when Pharaoh executed a prisoner on Pharaoh's birthday?

Although the Bible says that the Lord was with Joseph, his adversaries kept putting him in mortal danger. How could this be? Why doesn't the Lord's presence in someone's life prevent such hazards?

"Joseph, I Should Explain…"

Several people failed to help Joseph when he encountered hard times. Imagine you are one of these fair-weather friends:

- Joseph's eldest brother, Reuben

- Potiphar

- Pharaoh's cupbearer

Write a brief letter to Joseph, explaining what you did (and didn't do) to help in his time of need and why you did (or didn't) do it, and asking forgiveness for your failure as a friend.

____

____

____

____

____

____

What (if anything) did any of these characters do to "make it up" to Joseph? What *could* they have done?

____

____

____

How do you think Joseph felt about the betrayal of these people who could have helped him in time of need?

____

____

____

____

What is it that can make an apology authentic and meaningful instead of ringing hollow and seeming worthless?

____

____

____

____

What does your letter reveal about the human tendency to withdraw from someone in trouble? When have you been there for a friend in need? When have you failed to be the friend you should have been?

____

____

____

____

The Unseen Guest

During the Great Depression, many homes had plaques or needle-point wall-hangings with this traditional German blessing:

Christ is the head of this house,

The unseen guest at every meal,

The silent listener at every conversation.

It reminded the family that God was aware of their needs and shared their suffering, even in the most austere times.

Recall a difficult time when you needed to know this—perhaps the loss of a job, a marital breakdown, or a debilitating injury or disease. If you had seen Christ as your guest at every meal during this ordeal, what would you have said to him? What do you think he would have said to you? What evidence did you see that Christ had been with you, after the crisis had passed?

Who do you know in your congregation or another group who is passing through a tough time right now? How could you share this experience with this person?

Love That Doesn't Let Go

George Matheson was studying for the ministry at the University of Glasgow when he went blind at the age of twenty. His fiancée broke off their engagement because of it, and his sister cared for him while he completed his studies and began serving as a pastor in Edinburgh. Twenty years later, she accepted a proposal of marriage and moved away to start of family of her own. Alone again, Matheson penned the hymn, "O Love that Will Not Let Me Go" to affirm his conviction that God would care for him. It begins:

O Love that will not let me go,
I rest my weary soul in Thee;
I give Thee back the life I owe,
That in Thine ocean depths its flow
May richer, fuller be.

Matheson lived another quarter century to write many more hymns and to lecture at the leading universities of the United Kingdom.

What Christian song gives you confidence of the Lord's care in hard times? Which of the lyrics are the most meaningful to you? Why?

Closing Prayer

Lord, forgive us for not seeing that you are still with us when hard times come. We confess that we sometimes allow difficulties to blind us to your gracious love, yet we know your love sustains us. That is our heritage, just as it was Joseph's heritage, so we pray that you will encourage us to tell others about it. Be our guide and provider through prosperous times and hard times, gracious and faithful Lord. Amen.■

L 3

Ruth Makes a Choice

Ruth 1 — 2:3

Main Point

Hard times brought some significant changes to Ruth's life; at some point, hard times may call each of us to try a different path.

Background

Stories of economic refugees are often featured in today's news, but this is not a new phenomenon. Political unrest, war, and natural disaster have often forced people to migrate to other lands in search of food and shelter. This was true of Joseph's family nearly three thousand years ago and Ruth's family a few centuries later. Most people hope to wait out hard times, but when their troubles last for years, they must move or die. They must try a different way of life in a different place, even if they are aliens there. This was the predicament Ruth found herself in.

Before and After

Losses require us to make changes for the future, painful though they may be. For each of the events below, describe how someone might live before and after the event occurred:

	Before	**After**
Bankruptcy		
Divorce		
Death of spouse		
Loss of home		

Suppose someone tried to live exactly the same way after one of these events as before. What problems might this create? What is an example of someone you know who tried to do this?

____

____

____

____

____

I. **Read** Ruth 1:1–7.

Moab bordered the east side of the Dead Sea. The soil there was thin and rocky, suitable for grazing animals but little else. How do you suppose Elimelech felt about leaving the "land of milk and honey" for this? Why?

____

____

____

The Moabites were distant cousins of the Jews who had refused to help them conquer the land of Canaan, so they were barred from worshiping in Jewish synagogues or marrying Jewish people. Write three to five phrases describing how a Jew must have felt to live as a refugee among these impoverished kin.

____

____

____

____

Write three to five phrases describing how a Moabite may have felt to have prosperous relatives become squatters among the Moabites during hard times.

____

____

____

Why were Naomi's daughters-in-law more inclined to accompany her back to Canaan instead of staying in Moab with their own people?

How would the companionship of Orpah and Ruth help Naomi? How would they be an additional burden to her?

Naomi insisted that she was too old to make a fresh start, so why was she returning to her homeland?

Orpah decided to stay in Moab and seek help among her own people, while Ruth decided to go with Naomi to a land and people she did not know. Which choice involved more risk? Why?

III. Read Ruth 1:15–21.

Ruth's pledge of loyalty to Naomi (vv 16–17) is one of the most beloved passages of the Old Testament. Where have you heard it quoted? Why do you think it is so popular?

Naomi and her family had left Bethlehem more than a decade earlier, and now "the whole town was stirred" to see her return without her family (v 19). How do you think the townspeople would tend to treat her, considering her calamity?

Naomi told the people to stop calling her Naomi ("pleasant") and to use the name Mara ("bitter") instead. Why was she bitter? Toward whom or what was she bitter?

IV. Read Ruth 1:22 — 2:3.

Ruth took the initiative to forage for food as soon as the women reached Bethlehem. Why do you suppose she asked Naomi's permission before she went to the fields?

Jewish law directed gleaners to leave some grain for the poor to gather. Why then did Ruth hope to find one "in whose eyes I find favor" (v 2)? How was she at a disadvantage?

"I Had No Choice"

When hard times come, we may feel like helpless victims, yet we have choices to cope with our problems going forward. When Ruth's husband died and her mother-in-law decided to go back home, Ruth could have surrendered to the circumstances. Instead, she made some bold choices.

Here are some examples of life crises that could come your way. In each case, what choice could you make to cope with the problem?

Crisis	Choice
A tornado destroys your home	
You are diagnosed with cancer	
You are fired at age sixty	
Your daughter dies in combat	
Your car is repossessed	
Your son is arrested for dealing drugs	

Why do some people seem to thrive and stay positive in spite of crises, while others are knocked off-track and have a difficult time moving forward? Why do some people seem to experience one crisis after another, while others rarely seem to have major problems? What difference does faith make?

Change? Don't Be Silly!

Sometimes a crisis requires us to question our traditional way of doing things. An Ohio banker wrote in September 1931, "I am getting weary of depression talk and patent remedies. You hear it on all sides…. It all seems silly to me. Everything will work itself out without these radical changes."[1]

We now know that things would get worse before they got better. Hundreds of banks closed and millions of people lost their homes. With Franklin D. Roosevelt's inauguration in 1933, radical changes did come to banking laws and other areas. The nation climbed out of the Great Depression, but only after Americans set aside "business as usual" to try something new.

We don't know what would have happened to Ruth if she had followed Naomi's advice to go back to her family, her former religion, and her familiar ways of doing things. But Ruth didn't do that. She returned to her late husband's country, married one of her Jewish kinsmen, and became an ancestor of Jesus.

Recall a hard time your congregation faced. Did your church maintain its traditional way of doing things, or did you try something new? How did you seek God's guidance? What was the outcome?

Safer Than Any Known Way

During the Bankers' Panic of 1907–08, a lecturer at the London School of Economics wrote this:

And I said to the man who stood at the gate of the year: "Give me a light that I may tread safely into the unknown." And he replied: "Go out into the darkness and put your hand into the Hand of God. That shall be to you better than light and safer than a known way."[2]

Ruth did this. She left a familiar way of life and made a new beginning in a foreign country after her husband died. There God guided and blessed her choices. Your best future may lie in an unfamiliar place, too—a place that you might not even attempt to explore unless hard times required it.

Recall a time when necessity forced you to move to an unfamiliar place, live among unfamiliar people, or do an unfamiliar kind of work. What happened? What did God reveal to you through that experience?

Closing Prayer

God, thank you for giving us choices, even when circumstances seem to conspire against us. And thank you for your consistent presence with us in all that we face. Remind us of Ruth, who dared to seek a new life in the Promised Land despite all the heartaches that had come her way. You have always been faithful to us in the past, so give us courage to trust you for the future, whatever it might hold. Amen.∎

1. Benjamin Roth, *The Great Depression: A Diary* (New York: Public Affairs Press, 2009), 23.

2. "The Gate of the Year," accessed June 13, 2018, https://en.wikipedia.org/wiki/The_Gate_of_the_Year.

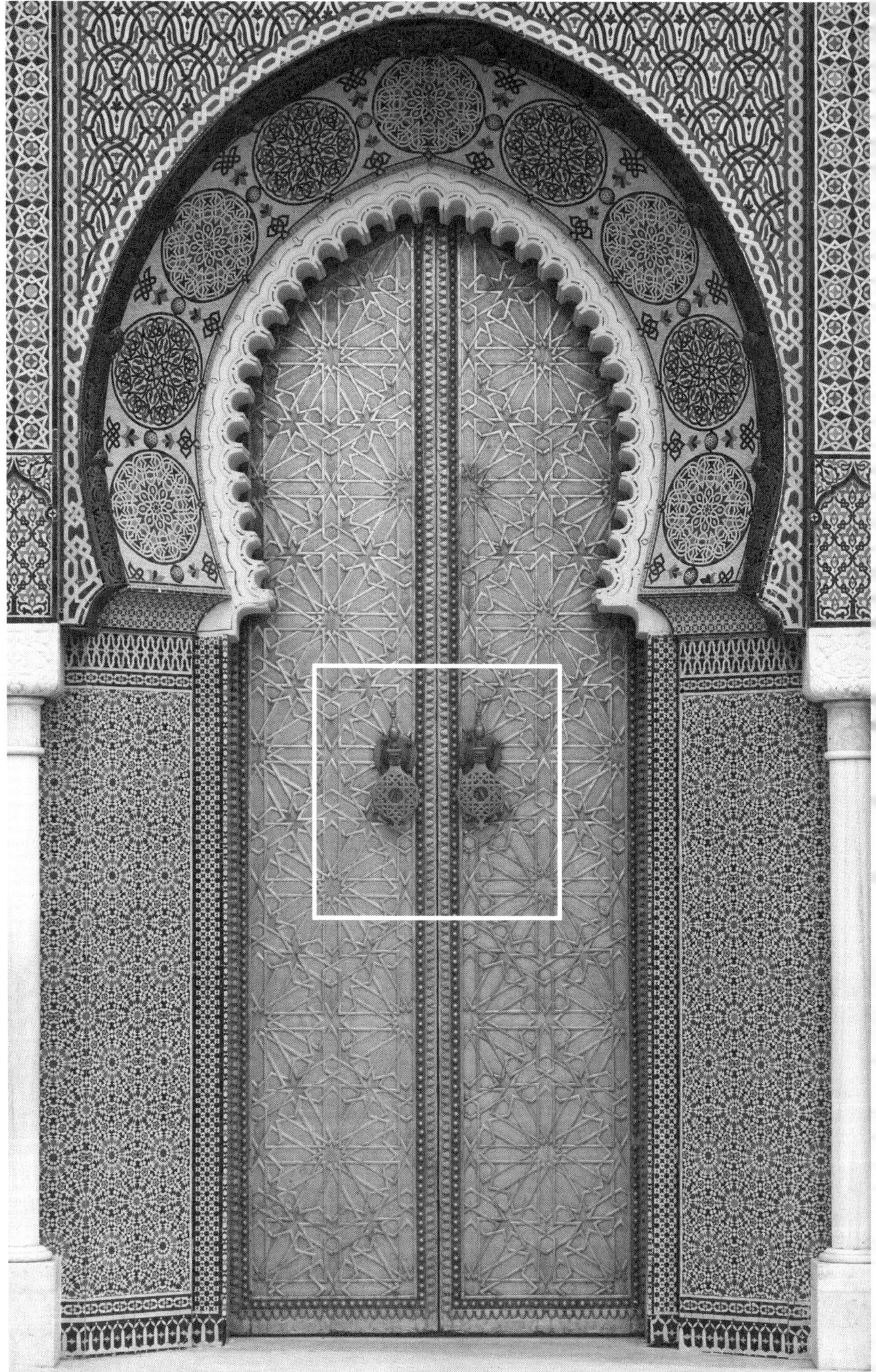

L4

Esther Risks Her Life

Esther 4:9–17; 5 — 6; 7:1–6, 10

Main Point

Esther took a significant risk when the lives of her people were threatened; hard times challenge us to take risks for others.

Background

When the Babylonians conquered Judah in the sixth century BC, they forced its inhabitants to return with them to Babylon (modern Iraq). One of these captives was Esther, who concealed her Jewish identity to became Babylon's new queen. When Esther's cousin Mordecai angered one of the king's lieutenants, the official decided to exact his revenge by getting a royal decree which would allow all Jews to be killed. This news so distressed Mordecai that he covered himself in sackcloth and mourned bitterly. Using her privileged position, Esther risked everything to help her people. She saved them—and, through them, God would save the world.

Whoever Saves One Life

One person can have a major impact on the lives of others. The story of Oskar Schindler demonstrates this. Schindler was a German businessman and member of the Nazi Party who is credited with saving the lives of 1,200 Jews during the Holocaust by employing them in his factories. He was initially motivated by profit, since the Jews provided free labor, but over time he came to care for these people and spent his fortune to keep them working for him and prevent them from being taken to concentration camps.

When World War II ended, Schindler was in danger of being arrested due to his membership in the Nazi Party. Before he fled, his workers presented him with a ring they had made him, with this inscription: "Whoever saves one life saves the world entire."

When have you seen one person take action that had a positive effect on multiple lives? Why did this person do it? How is this person remembered today for what he or she did?

In what sorts of positions today do individual people have the power to make decisions that will positively impact or even save many lives?

I. **Read** Esther 4:9–17.

Mordecai sent word of the imminent massacre of the Jews and asked Esther to plead with the king to rescind the order, but she said palace protocol did not allow this. Only someone summoned by the king could talk with him. Have you ever made an urgent appeal for help and been told you had to follow certain procedures? How did you feel about that? What did you do?

Mordecai warned Esther, "Do not think that because you are in the king's house you…will escape" (v 13). What do you suppose the king would have done when he learned that his wife was a Jew? Why?

II. Read Esther 5.

Esther and her attendants had fasted for three days before she approached the king. How would that have affected Esther? What did it demonstrate to God?

____

____

____

____

Esther did not immediately raise the issue of the king's decree against the Jews. Rather, she invited him and Haman to a banquet the next day. Why?

____

____

____

"But all of this gives me no satisfaction as long as I see that Jew Mordecai sitting at the king's gate," Haman said (v 13). Why did Mordecai's presence affect Haman more than the queen's banquet invitation?

____

____

____

____

III. Read Esther 6:1–13.

A bout of insomnia reminded the king of Mordecai's loyalty. Have you ever used a sleepless night to reflect on how God has blessed your life? Describe the experience.

When the king asked Haman what he should do for a man he wished to honor, Haman thought that he himself would be the recipient. How is this consistent with what we have already seen of Haman's self-assessment?

The Bible does not say why Haman's wife and friends predicted that he could not prevail against Mordecai and other Jews. Why do you suppose they reached this conclusion?

IV. Read Esther 6:14 — 7:6, 10.

The king offered to give Esther anything she asked, even half of his kingdom. This was quite generous, considering that women seldom owned land in the ancient world. Why do you think the king was so generous with her?

"Grant me my life…. And spare my people," Esther said (v 3). Why would this statement have surprised the king and Haman?

What risks did Esther take by doing all of this? What if the king had defended Haman's actions?

Escalation of Hatred

In Esther's story, genocide seemed to spring unexpectedly from a trivial event, but this is seldom true. Ethnic hatred usually escalates over a long period of time before something triggers a violent response. The good news is that courageous people can identify and stop the escalation of hatred before it explodes in violence. The following chart (based on Nazi anti-Semitism) shows how hatred against a particular ethnic group can escalate. See how many of these stages can you identify, directed against a particular ethnic or social group:

Stage of Hatred	Action against Ethnic Group
Ridicule	
Partiality	
Unpunished Crimes	
Hate Speech by Public Figures	
Denial of Constitutional Rights	
Isolation	
Genocide	

In our society, what groups tend to be the target of hatred by others? Why?

If you have been the target of this kind of hatred, how did (or do) you respond? What could an individual do to stop the escalation of hate at each stage, whether or not that person was an actual target of the hatred?

Which Risk Is Greater?

When Mordecai asked Esther to intercede with the king, she initially weighed the risk—and declined. But after Mordecai pointed out that she would also be a target of the genocide decree, she reconsidered the risk—and agreed. What risks would you have if you tried to help these people in your community? What if you don't help them?

People Having Hard Times	Risks If I Help Them	Risks If I Don't Help Them
Unemployed		
Homeless		
Drug Addicts		
Prostitutes		
Illegal Immigrants		

When have you initially declined to get involved in a situation but then changed your mind later? What caused your change of mind? What was the outcome of the whole process?

In what kinds of situations is our involvement "worth the risk"—even if that risk means we will not be guaranteed to succeed, receive a proper return on our investment, or even know for sure how things turn out?

Just Outside Our Door

American songwriter Stephen Foster penned these words in 1854:

Let us pause in life's pleasures and count its many tears
While we all sup sorrow with the poor;
There's a song that will linger forever in our ears;
Oh! Hard times, come again no more.

While we seek mirth and beauty and music light and gay
There are frail forms fainting at the door;
Though their voices are silent, their pleading looks will say
Oh! Hard times, come again no more.

Chorus:
Tis the song, the sigh of the weary;
Hard times, hard times, come again no more;
Many days you have lingered around my cabin door;
Oh! Hard times, come again no more.

Foster's song echoes Jesus' Parable of the Rich Man and Lazarus (Luke 16:19–31). Compare and contrast how the song and the parable describe relations between the "haves" and "have nots." Describe your relationships with neighbors who are having hard times.

Closing Prayer

God, we confess that we sometimes hesitate to help people having hard times because we are preoccupied with our own problems or, like Esther, we fear the risk of helping them. Thank you for giving Esther the courage to act. We pray that you will give us a portion of that courage, as well. Show us how to help others bear their burdens, and help us realize when you are calling us to act. Amen. ∎

L 5

Persecuted for Jesus

Acts 5:12–42

Main Point

Despite imprisonment and beating, the apostles continued to faithfully share the news of new life in Christ; we too can proclaim Christ in the face of opposition.

Background

Peter and the apostles were crystal-clear on the focus of their allegiance: they would obey God by continuing to teach in the name of Jesus Christ, regardless of the persecution it might bring them. Some in the Sanhedrin were furious and wanted to have the apostles executed. But the Sanhedrin eventually decided to have the apostles flogged and released, again warning them not to speak in the name of Jesus. Luke is clear that such threats did nothing to stop or even slow down the apostles; in public and in private they continued to boldly teach and proclaim the good news that Jesus is the Messiah.

Everyday Obedience

Even though the circumstances may differ, we all face situations where obedience seems to present a dilemma. For each situation described below, ask yourself: Would I obey? *Should* I obey? Why? What would I obey—the law, the "sense" of the situation, or something else? What further details would I need to know in order to make a decision?

1. You are driving on an Interstate where there is a sixty-five-mile-an-hour speed limit. As you drive right at the speed limit you notice that a steady stream of traffic is continuously passing you. You think about speeding up to seventy or seventy-five to move more smoothly with the flow of other cars.

____

____

2. You are going to be making a vacation trip to a country that has a regulation against importing Bibles. It saddens you that the citizens of this land cannot obtain free access to the Scriptures, so you take along twenty small paperback Bibles. Will you declare them as you pass through customs?

____

____

3. You are a cashier in a neighborhood market. Your boss tells you that you are to ring up an extra dollar on several large sales each hour. How do you handle the situation?

____

____

I. **Read** Acts 5:12–16.

What was it that seemed to draw people to the apostles and, ultimately, to Jesus? Does this same sort of attraction happen today? Explain.

Why might some people have hesitated to join this group of Christians? Why do people today hesitate to become part of God's people, the church? What do you think God thinks about it? How should we respond?

II. Read Acts 5:17–26.

What motivated the high priest and his associates to jail the apostles? Why was it so important to the Lord that the word of "this new life" (v 20) continue to be preached? How does God act today to ensure that the word gets out?

____

____

____

____

In this story, an angel of the Lord miraculously released the apostles from jail so they could continue preaching. But in the rest of Acts, God did not always miraculously release people from jail or protect them from harm—nor does God always do so today. Why the discrepancy?

____

____

____

III. Read Acts 5:27–42.

What reasons did Peter and the other apostles give for their commitment to keep on teaching in the name of Jesus? How do these same reasons apply in our own time and context?

____

____

____

____

The members of the Sanhedrin felt obedience to and enforcement of Jewish Law to be of utmost importance. They had their own understanding of God and God's ways. They believed they were right in what they were doing. Were they being as obedient as we would expect of people in their position? How could things have been different?

Peter and the apostles sensed a call to be God's messengers or ambassadors. They placed God first in their loyalties—ahead of the Roman government and ahead of the council of Jews they were facing here. Were they wise and practical in their obedience? Did their actions represent total commitment to the way of Christ? Why or why not?

Gamaliel had a cooler head than the other members of the Sanhedrin. He was known and respected for his wisdom. In taking his stand in the Sanhedrin he was being obedient to his own insights and commitments and his understanding of the apostles. Do you feel that if Gamaliel had been closer to the Lord, he would have taken an even bolder stand? Explain.

How did the Sanhedrin ultimately respond to the apostles? And how did the apostles, in turn, respond? How often do we rejoice in suffering for the name of Christ? How often do we even suffer for this reason—period? Explain.

Despite the repeated warnings and even receiving a flogging, the apostles refused to quit "teaching and proclaiming the good news that Jesus is the Messiah" (v 42). What things tend to discourage God's people from sharing about Jesus? Why might we seem to lack the power, the passion, and the sense of urgency the apostles had?

Obedience Analysis

Here are some questions we might face when making decisions of obedience. How might you respond to each, and why? How would your response change depending on the situation, and why? How important would you consider each question, and why?

When authorities disagree on their demands for obedience, how do we choose which authority to obey?

How much obedience does a person have a right to ask for? Should obedience be expected if it causes intense pain? What if it costs great sums of money? What if it even results in death?

What exactly will my obedience cause me to have to do? Is the action I must take important? Is it right or wrong?

Whom will I be supporting if I obey? Whom will I be against?

How do virtues such as love, duty, honesty, integrity, wisdom, and faithfulness fit in with my obedience or disobedience in this case?

A Story of Obedience

Dietrich Bonhoeffer grew up in Berlin and studied theology there. After an assistant pastorate in Barcelona, he taught in London and America, and later served at a German seminary. In the late 1930s he wrote *The Cost of Discipleship,* a stirring attack on "cheap grace."

In 1939 Bonhoeffer was on a lecture trip through America when war broke out in Europe. He was urged by many to remain in the United States, where his theological and ecumenical work could proceed un-hampered. But he felt that he should return to his homeland and join the small movement resisting Hitler.

In Germany, Bonhoeffer was forbidden by the government to lecture, write, or preach. Nevertheless, he found ways to travel throughout the country and support Christians in their opposition to Hitler. He was finally arrested, cut off from outside contact, and eventually hanged on April 9, 1945. Among his last words were, "This is the end—for me the beginning of life."

Even obedience in matters that seem small can be an encouragement to those who seek to obey the Lord and faithfully follow his call. How does your commitment to God compare to that of Dietrich Bonhoeffer? to that of the apostles?

We sometimes think of obedience only in terms of dramatic, world-shaking actions. When we hear such stories, they inspire us. But it is important for us to be ready to obey in the small, everyday situations of life. Think about some of the little acts of obedience you might be faced with during the coming week. Maybe it will be a matter of saying no to an old, troublesome habit again. Perhaps it will be a matter of going the second mile in relating to a coworker who really "pushes your buttons." Or it could be a matter of walking away from a conversation that turns into gossip or includes language that is not edifying. List your ideas here:

What can obedience in the "little" things indicate about our obedience (or potential obedience) in weightier matters?

What does Matthew 25:14–30 have to teach us about obedience? In what "hard places" is God trusting you to obey?

Closing Prayer

God, some of the hard times we face are due to our own choices. But regardless of the reason, you are faithful to walk the journey of life with us. Sometimes that journey includes hard times. We thank you for the comfort and strength brought by your life-giving presence. When hard times result from our commitment to taking a stand for you, help us to rejoice that we have been counted worthy of suffering for your name. Amen. ■

L 6

Peter Escapes from Prison

Acts 12:1–19a

Main Point

Acts 12 describes Peter's deliverance from prison; in the midst of perilous life situations, deliverance can come through prayer and sometimes even through miraculous means.

Background

During the reign of Herod Agrippa, the leaders of the young Christian church faced persecution. Even while the believers rapidly reached out in ever-widening circles, we read in Acts 12 of the martyrdom of James, the brother of John, and also the arrest of Peter. It is likely that Peter also was headed for execution as a part of Herod's campaign to please the Jewish religious leaders. With Peter kept under heavy guard, the church gathered to pray for him. But at night, as Peter slept between two soldiers, an angel of the Lord led him on a miraculous escape. Prison walls could not separate Peter from God's ever-present help.

A Story of Opposition

Florence Nightingale was born in 1820 and spent most of her childhood in in an upper-class home and a society where women were not encouraged to pursue careers—expected instead to have limited education and be protected from the rougher elements of life. By the age of seventeen, she was hearing a voice from God telling her that she had a mission, which she pursued despite opposition from those around her. She found her way into the nursing field, which had never been open to women. In the 1850s Nightingale volunteered her services in the Crimean War, making herself so useful that she could not be ignored. Eventually she ended up directing all nursing operations on the Crimean front. Following the war she fought to encourage professional nurses' training for women, helped to improve health conditions in the British army and sanitary conditions in hospitals, and worked to develop the nursing profession.

Think about friends, family members, or people you have known in the church who persisted in their faith despite hard times. How have some come through economic challenges? How have some overcome the limitations of poor health? How have some faced opposition to the work of the church?

I. Read Acts 12:1–5.

Why would the Jews be pleased about James being murdered? Why would Herod be pleased that the Jews were pleased? Why would Herod delay Peter's trial and potential execution?

James, one of the "inner circle" of disciples (along with Peter and John), was killed, while Peter ended up being freed from prison and death. Why the difference? What factors might have played a part in these different outcomes?

Peter was placed under heavy guard. Why the excessive number of soldiers? Was there something else the church should have done, or was prayer enough? How do we know when God expects us to do more than pray?

II. Read Acts 12:6–11.

What does the fact that Peter was asleep in the prison imply about Peter's state of mind at that point? Think of a time you were going through a trying situation. How did God enable you to relax or experience peace in spite of the circumstances you were experiencing?

God had an angel tap Peter and speak to him, removed Peter's chains and opened the jail doors, and kept the soldiers from noticing any of it. Why do you think God chose this method rather than, say, an earthquake, or instead of keeping Peter out of prison in the first place?

Why do you think the angel left Peter when they got out into the city streets? How does God give us grace and strength in proportion to our need at specific points in time?

Why do you think it took Peter so long to realize that he was truly free? What things sometimes keep us from recognizing God's work on our behalf or make us skeptical that God is the one behind it? When have you looked back on a situation and realized that God was with you and at work the whole time?

III. Read Acts 12:12–19a.

What do you think the believers at Mary's house were praying for? What else might they have been doing? Why do you think they were slow to believe that it was actually Peter at the door?

Why do you think Peter just made a brief appearance at Mary's house and then hurried off to "another place" (v 17)? Didn't he trust that God would keep him safe? Explain.

How did Herod respond to Peter's escape? What did Peter's newfound freedom potentially mean for Herod? for the church?

We should not be surprised when God answers our prayers—he is at work in all situations that concern his children, whether or not we see it. As you recall the events reported in Acts 12:1–19a, consider what the following people might say about how to get out of trouble and how to deal with persecution.

James, the brother of John. Among the original twelve disciples, James and John were in a circle of men especially close to Jesus. They were probably outspoken and vigorous in their leadership of the young church. When Herod Agrippa began persecuting Christian leaders, James was executed.

Peter. Peter was imprisoned under heavy guard, likely headed for execution. Then God intervened, sending an angel to miraculously lead Peter to freedom.

The Church. The Christians in the young church at Jerusalem must have been stricken with fear when King Herod began persecuting their leaders. But they did not sit idly by.

How do you think James would respond to questions about how to deal with persecution?

How would Peter talk about dealing with persecution and finding help?

How did the church respond to opposition? What might they suggest to us when we need help?

God's Intervention

Sometimes God calls for persistence in a certain situation, and sometimes he closes a door or asks us to pursue a different opportunity (see Acts 16:6–10). We depend on God for saving miracles, for the strength to endure, and also for the wisdom to know when it's time for a change.

Think about the story of Peter's escape. Should we always expect God to come to our aid and do the miraculous? Explain.

Christians pray often, about many things. But what do we do in times of doubt or when answers don't seem to come? Do we recognize the positive answers to our prayers when they come? Why or why not?

In the face of apparent failures of some church programs, how persistent should we be in our attempts to win some people to the Lord, or in other situations where the answers we seek seem to be delayed?

As followers of Christ, we have the Holy Spirit to guide us and instruct us. He can help us know what is best to do in each situation. How can we develop and effectively use such "Spirit discernment"?

Sometimes we make bad decisions or poor choices that cause tough times. But even when this is not the case, we can be impacted by the "brokenness" of our world (Rom 8:19–22) and the choices others make as a part of their free will. How do we tell which principles are in operation in a particular situation? Do we even need to know? Explain.

One response to tough times that is definitely not appropriate is to do nothing. We may be asked by God to take action at different levels. Praying for God's will to be accomplished through us is always appropriate. The only action that is definitely too little is doing nothing at all. How do you respond to this idea, and why?

Closing Prayer

Lord, we have earnestly prayed for your help in the lives of many people, and others have earnestly prayed for us. Give us discernment as we pray and act, so we might know without a doubt that you are at work. Your Word tells us that Jesus endured the shame of the cross because of the joy of following you. With your joy and strength, help us to move forward in the midst of hard times. Amen. ∎